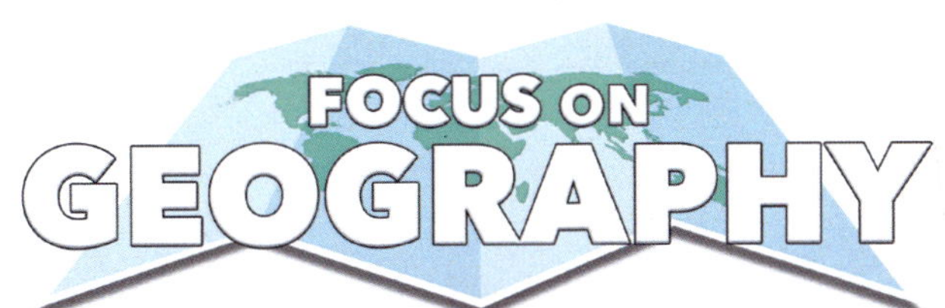

Focus on China

Heather C. Hudak

A Crabtree Forest Book

Crabtree Publishing
crabtreebooks.com

Author: Heather C. Hudak

Series research and development: Janine Deschenes

Editorial director: Kathy Middleton

Editor: Ellen Rodger, Janine Deschenes

Proofreader: Melissa Boyce

Design: Katherine Berti

Photo research: Ellen Rodger, Katherine Berti

IMAGE CREDITS

Flickr
Gary Todd: p. 20 (bottom left)

Shutterstock
amnat30: p. 41 (center right), 33 (top), 41 (center right)
Anton_Ivanov: p. 41 (bottom left)
Barnaby Chambers: p. 14 (bottom right), 37 (center left)
beibaoke: p. 18 (top and bottom left), 21 (center left)
B.Zhou: p. 45 (top left)
chinahbzyg: p. 31 (center), 40 (bottom), 45 (top right)
Danny Ye: p. 19 (vase center right)
Grigvovan: p. 31 (top), 32 (bottom left), 40 (center)
GuoZhongHua: p. 28 (top)
humphery: p. 30 (bottom), 32 (bottom right and top), 33 (bottom)
Hung Chung Chih: p. 10 (bottom right), 42 (bottom)
junrong: p. 28 (center)
Kylie Nicholson: p. 35 (top)
liyuhan: p. 30 (center)
LMspencer: p. 1
On the road again: p. 34 (bottom left)
Shan_shan: p. 18 (bottom right), 19 (top right)
Songquan Deng: p. 26 (bottom left)
SIHASAKPRACHUM: p. 22 (top)
Steve Heap: p. 38 (top)
Tao Jiang: p. 34 (bottom right)
testing: p. 30 (top)
TonyV3112: p. 34 (top), 45 (center right)
Vladimir Zhoga: p. 13 (inset top right)
windmoon: p. 3 (left), 39 (bottom), 41 (bottom right)
Yury Birukov: p. 35 (bottom)

Wikimedia Commons
张青云: p. 29 (top)
Anne S.K. Brown Military Collection—98th_Foot_at_Chinkiang: p. 25 (bottom left)
anonymous potter from the Jingdezhen imperial kilns: p. 23 (bottom left)
Digitized by NPM; image is directly from Shuge: p. 17 (right), 23 (top)
Dong Fang: p. 29 (bottom)
Gary Todd: p. 22 (center right)
Li Ung Bin, Outlines of Chinese History, shanghai 1914: p. 17 (bottom center)
ocw.mit.edu:ans7870:21f:21f.027:opium_wars_01:ow1_gallery:pages:1841_0792_nemesis_jm_nmm.htm: p. 24–25 (center)
Seed, John, Hubert Vos, Court Painter of Empres Dowager Cixi, Arts of Asia, Jan:Feb 2015: p. 24 (bottom left)
Photo by Rio V. De Sieux: p. 26 (top)
unknown author: p. 24 (bottom center)
verdammelt: p. 15 (top right)
www.bbshuaxia.cn:xia:2010-09-08:1017.html: p. 20 (top right)

All other images from Shutterstock

Crabtree Publishing

crabtreebooks.com 800-387-7650

In Canada: We acknowledge the financial support of the Government of Canada through the Canada Book Fund for our publishing activities.

Hardcover 978-1-0398-4291-5
Paperback 978-1-0398-4299-1
Ebook (pdf) 978-1-0398-4306-6
Epub 978-1-0398-4312-7

Published in Canada
Crabtree Publishing
616 Welland Avenue
St. Catharines, Ontario
L2M 5V6

Published in the United States
Crabtree Publishing
347 Fifth Avenue
Suite 1402-145
New York, New York, 10016

Library and Archives Canada Cataloguing in Publication
Available at Library and Archives Canada

Library of Congress Cataloging-in-Publication Data
Available at the Library of Congress

Printed in the USA/062024/CG20240201

Contents

Introduction

In Beijing, both ancient wonders and contemporary ways of life meld together. The city dates back about 3,000 years. It has been the capital of China for eight centuries. Today, with nearly 22 million residents, Beijing is the second most **populous** city in the People's **Republic** of China. It is also the eighth most populous city in the world.

Daily life is fast-paced in Beijing. Workdays are long, and people have limited time off. Grandparents often care for their grandchildren while their parents are at work. However, life slows down at night. Beijing has many modern shops, restaurants, and nightclubs where people can spend their leisure time.

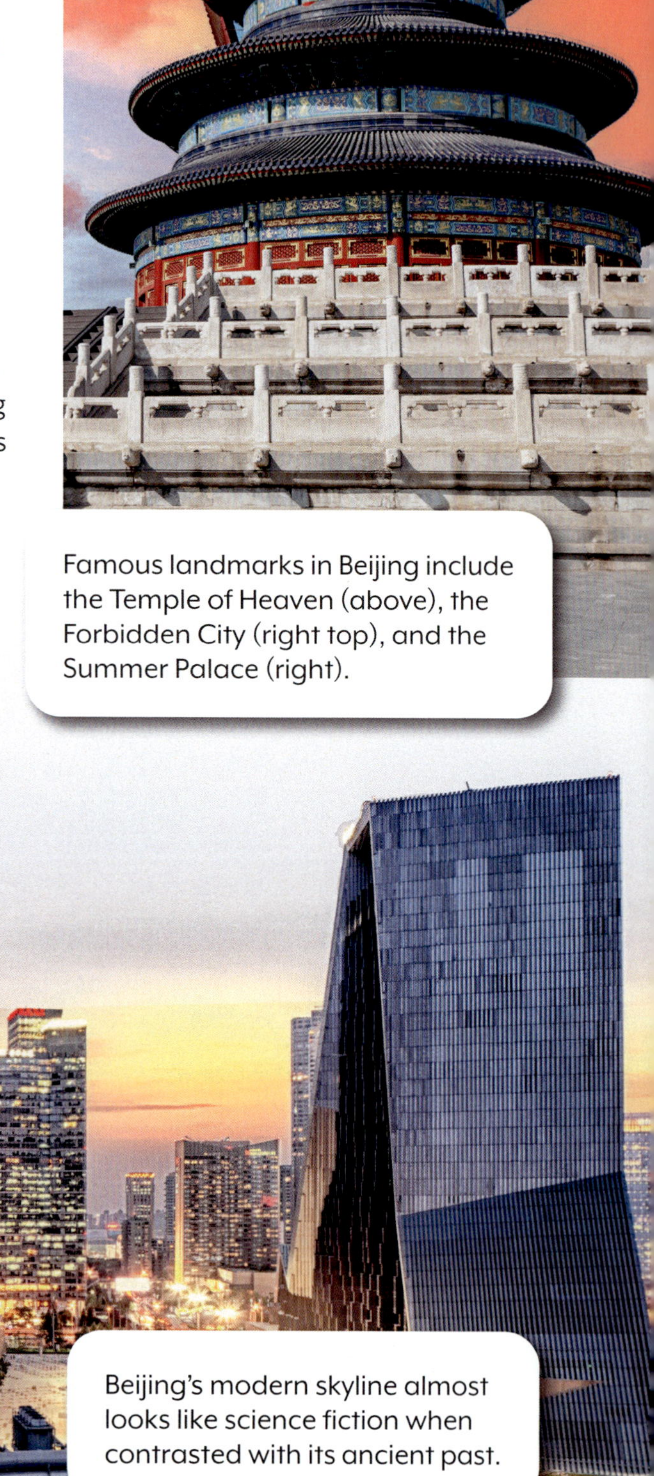

Famous landmarks in Beijing include the Temple of Heaven (above), the Forbidden City (right top), and the Summer Palace (right).

Beijing's modern skyline almost looks like science fiction when contrasted with its ancient past.

Traditional courtyard homes are called siheyuan in Beijing. The alleys surrounding them are called hutongs.

Battling Smoggy Skies

Since the mid-1900s, Beijing has become highly **industrialized**. As a result, air quality is poor due to heavy pollution. Smog often fills the skies. It can be so bad that school and outdoor activities, such as sports, are sometimes canceled. It's also common to see people wearing masks as they go about their day in an effort to protect their lungs from damage. Beijing's fast **economic** growth in the late 1900s led to the streets becoming overcrowded with vehicles. Traffic is tangled, with heavy **carbon emissions**. To help solve the problem, Beijing has used a license lottery since 2011 to limit the number of vehicles on the road. This means just a small percent of drivers can win a chance to register their vehicle.

Public Transport

Most people in Beijing rely on public transportation systems to get around the city. There are hundreds of bus routes and more than two dozen subway lines. They are continually improved to help combat the growing traffic and transportation problem.

Despite the push to modernize the city, Beijing is home to some of the oldest and most important historic sites in the world. In old Beijing, mazes of winding alleyways called *hutongs* surround *siheyuan*, or neighborhoods of traditional courtyard residences—some of them built in the late 1200s. Many of these were destroyed over the last century to make way for newer buildings. But the Chinese government has now designated some as culturally protected areas.

Mountains to Deserts

China is the largest country on the continent of Asia and the fourth-largest country in the world in terms of size. Only Russia, Canada, and the United States are larger. China is nearly the size of the entire European continent. The **topography** of China includes everything from mountains to lowlands and plateaus to deserts and deltas.

China is located in East Asia. It shares borders with 14 countries—Russia, North Korea, and Mongolia to the north, India, Bhutan, Nepal, Laos, Myanmar, Vietnam, and Pakistan to the south, and Afghanistan, Tajikistan, Kyrgyzstan, and Kazakhstan to the west. The East China Sea and Yellow Sea border China to the east. To the southeast, China is bordered by the South China Sea.

China has the second-largest population in the world. It accounts for about one-fifth of the total global population. The country is considered **ethnically homogenous**, meaning that the majority of people share a common culture and heritage. However, there are many ethnic and language groups across the country. The **Han people** are the largest of these groups, and the Beijing **dialect** of Mandarin is the country's official language.

The rainbow mountains of Quilian are in Zhangye National Geopark in Gansu, a province in northwest China. They get their color from the mineral deposits in the sandstone surface.

Farmland in Anhui, a province in eastern China

Camels being led through the Singing Sand Dunes in Dunhuang, northwestern Gansu province.

AT A GLANCE

- **OFFICIAL NAME:** The People's Republic of China (PRC)
- **NATIONAL CAPITAL:** Beijing
- **POPULATION:** 1.412 billion
- **OFFICIAL LANGUAGE:** Mandarin Chinese
- **LAND AREA:** 3.693 million square miles (9.567 million sq. km)

CHAPTER 1 The Land

From an **administrative** perspective, China is divided into 23 provinces. China claims Taiwan as a province but does not govern it. It also governs four municipalities: Beijing, Shanghai, Chongqing, and Tianjin. These cities are so large that they have been given the same rights as the provinces, and they report directly to the central government. China also has five **autonomous** regions. These are places where the culture, customs, and language are distinct from the Han people that make up the majority of the country. In addition, China has two special administrative regions: Hong Kong and Macau.

The Crescent Moon Spring in north-central Gansu province is an oasis in the Gobi Desert. An oasis is an area in a desert where water and plants are found.

Geographic Regions

In addition to administrative divisions, China is separated into three key geographic regions: eastern, central, and western. Eastern China consists mainly of plains and lowlands. This region is situated along coastlines and is known for its fertile soils. As a result, it has the best agricultural lands. The western region is the largest, and it accounts for more than 60 percent of China's land. The landscape there is one of extremes. It consists mainly of mountains and hills, but there are also deserts and plateaus. This area has very little farmable land because it is either too high, too cold, or too dry. The landlocked central region lies between the western and eastern regions. It is rich in natural resources.

The eastern Pamir Mountains near Kashgar, in the northwest Xinjiang Uyghur Autonomous Region of China

These wheat fields are located near the Qinling-Huaihe Line that unofficially divides northern and southern China. Regions to the north are temperate in climate and regions to the south are subtropical and tropical.

Land and People

Most people in China live in the east, where the land is lower. The eastern region accounts for just 10 percent of the land, but it is home to 34 percent of China's population. The mountainous western region is sparsely populated, accounting for less than 30 percent of the population. Despite the country's massive population, large parts of the land remain rural, and about 50 percent of the population lives in these areas. Due to the country's massive size, the population **density** in China is lower than many European countries and other countries in Asia. The most heavily populated areas are in Beijing and Shenyang and along the Yangtze and Yellow River valleys, the Xi Jiang River delta, and the Sichuan Basin.

A village on the Li River in Guangxi. The South China Karst mountains are a group that spans four provinces in China, including these in Guangxi. They are a **UNESCO World Heritage Site**. Karst is a type of rock landform.

Shenyang is a city of 9 million and the provincial capital of the northeast coastal province of Liaoning. It is a megalopolis, or super city. China has an estimated 13 megalopolises, although as of 2023, only 10 are recognized as such.

A farmer works in the terraced rice paddies in Longji, in Guangxi Zhuang Autonomous Region (GZAR) in south China. The Longsheng, or Lonji Rice Terraces, called the Dragon's Backbone, were built along the slope of the Li River 650 years ago.

Closer Look

Hong Kong is both a city and a SAR. It was a colony of the British Empire from 1842 until 1997 when it was transferred to China.

Hong Kong, Macau, and Taiwan

Hong Kong was a British territory until 1997, when it was **ceded** to China. In 1999, Macau was returned to China by the Portuguese. Today, both Hong Kong and Macau are special administrative regions (SARs) of China. They have separate political, legal, and economic systems from China. Because their systems are so different from the rest of the country, both SARs experience tensions with China and sometimes face limitations on their political freedoms. It is not a SAR, but the island of Taiwan has been governed independently from mainland China since 1949. Although Taiwan views itself as distinct from China, it has the official name of Republic of China (ROC) and the government of the People's Republic of China (PRC) considers Taiwan to be one of its provinces. Relations between the two have declined as China seeks to reunify, or join, Taiwan with the rest of the country.

Taiwan, known officially as the Republic of China, includes a main island and 167 smaller islands.

Major Waterways

China has more than 50,000 rivers. Most rivers flow from west to east and drain into the Pacific Ocean. A small percentage drain into the Indian Ocean or Arctic Ocean. The three main rivers are the Huang He, or Yellow River, the Xi, and the Yangtze, which is the longest river in China and the third longest in the world. China also has about 2,800 natural lakes and many artificial lakes, or reservoirs. Most of the larger lakes are found in the Qinghai-Tibet Plateau. Poyang Lake is China's largest freshwater lake, and Qinghai Lake is the largest saltwater lake.

A road winds through Tianmen Mountain in China's south-central Hunan province. The east and south of the province are surrounded by several mountain ranges.

Notable Peaks

Mountains are a dominant feature in much of China's landscape. It is home to seven of the top 12 highest mountains and has almost 12,000 named mountains. There are five key mountain ranges: the Tian Shan that stretch from east to west across the north, the Qilian Shan in west-central China, and the Himalayas, the Kunlun Shan, and the Hengduan Shan in the south. Standing 29,032 feet (8,849 m) high, Mount Everest, which sits along the border of China and Nepal in the Tibet Autonomous Region, is the highest mountain in the world. K2, the second-highest mountain in the world, is also located partly in China.

The Yellow River is the second-longest river in China, at 3,395 miles (5,464 km) long. It flows through seven provinces and two autonomous regions before emptying in the Bohai Sea. It is considered the birthplace of ancient China.

Nearly 5 million Tibetans live in the Qinghai-Tibet Plateau and surrounding mountains, which include the Himalayan, Kunlun, and Altun ranges. Despite the high altitude, these people have adapted to living with low levels of oxygen.

Roof of the World

At about 14,800 feet (4,500 m) above sea level, the Tibetan Plateau, or Qinghai-Tibet Plateau, towers over southwestern China. Also known as the roof of the world, it stretches across 965,000 square miles (2,500,000 sq. km), making it the highest and largest plateau in the world. It covers all of Tibet and much of Qinghai province. It also reaches into the western part of Sichuan province and southern Xinjiang.

Disappearing Forests

Centuries of farming, coupled with the rapid growth of the nation in the mid-1900s, led to the destruction of China's forests. Vast numbers of trees were cut down to make way for more farmland and growing urban areas. **Deforestation** led to soil erosion and **desertification**. Since the 1990s, China has worked hard to reverse the damage through various forestry programs. Forestry land has increased from about 17 percent to more than 23 percent.

Natural Resources

China has an abundance of minerals, but much of its potential remains undeveloped. Petroleum is found in large quantities in northeast China, along with large deposits of coal, which is also common in north-central China. Owing to the vast network of rivers, China boasts valuable **hydroelectric resources**, especially in the southwest.

China is one of the largest producers of gold and magnesium. Iron ore is common in most provinces across China, and the country is the third-largest producer in the world. It is also a leading producer of aluminum, antimony, barite, magnesium, natural graphite, rare earths, steel, tungsten, and zinc.

Diverse Climates

Climate varies widely across the country due to the diverse topography. No other country in the world faces a greater difference in temperature from north to south. Parts of northern China dip well below freezing in the cold winter months. In the summer, they are hot and steamy. **Monsoon** season takes place between April and September in southern China, which also has a more tropical climate compared to the moderate climate of China's mountainous areas. Most parts of the country are very hot in July and August, while January is the coldest month of the year. Much like the temperature, rainfall decreases from south to north. **Climate change** is a major threat to China's coastal cities due to more frequent and intense coastal flooding, sea-level rise, severe weather events, storm surges, coastal erosion, and saltwater **intrusion**.

China gets about 21 typhoons per year, mostly in east, central, and southern areas from April to November. Typhoons are strong, spiraling storms, like hurricanes, that occur in the northwest Pacific Ocean.

Plants and Animals

China's varying landscapes, topography, and climates are home to a rich diversity of plant and animal life. The country has more than 31,000 plant species, many of them found nowhere else on Earth. Examples include the Chinese cypress, Cathay silver fir, golden larch, Fujian cypress, dove tree, and the metasequoia, which is one of the oldest and rarest plants on the planet. China accounts for nearly one-eighth of the world's total plant species, making it one of the countries with the most abundant plant life.

Thanks in large part to the broad diversity of plant life, animal life is also very abundant in China. With about 7,500 different types of animals, the country accounts for a large amount of the world's animal species. There are also many species that are native to China, including giant pandas, red pandas, Chinese giant salamanders, golden-haired monkeys, Chinese sturgeon, Tibetan macaques, Chinese red-headed centipedes, South China tigers, golden pheasants, white-flag dolphins, and Chinese alligators.

Monsoon flooding in Kunming, the capital of southwest Yunnan province

A eucalyptus forest in China where trees are **genetically altered** to grow faster and thicker with more disease resistance, so they can be harvested quicker. Conservationists blame these forests for depleting soils and increasing the risk of wildfires.

The Chinese pangolin is a critically endangered "anteater" native to southern China. It is a protected species threatened by poaching and the illegal trade in wildlife. Some people eat its meat and its scales are used as an ingredient in traditional medicine.

A giant panda sleeps on a tree branch at a wildlife reserve in Sichuan province.

The Lizhong Water Forest Park in the city of Xinghua in Jiangsu province is a park planted with thousands of metasequoia trees adapted to living in water. The park was created as an "oxygen bar" for visitors from the crowded city. Climate change in Jiangsu has increased temperatures, making parks like this important.

The Chinese, or Yangtze, alligator is also known as the "muddy dragon." It lives in the Yangtze and its tributaries. It is considered one of the most endangered alligators in the world as habitat loss and hunting has reduced its numbers.

CHAPTER 2 Becoming China

China is one of the oldest countries in the world. Chinese civilizations date back at least 4,000 years. However, there is evidence to suggest that humans have been in the area for much longer—hundreds of thousands of years, in fact. In 1927, archaeologists discovered the skull of an ancient human near Beijing. Peking Man lived in the area between 700,000 to 300,000 years ago. Another skull discovered in Yuanmou in 1965 dates back about 1.7 million years.

Neolithic Period

Settled communities began to take shape during the **Neolithic** period, between 7000 B.C.E. and 1700 B.C.E. They were most commonly found along major river systems, such as the Yellow and the Yangtze rivers. Neolithic people developed stone tools and began farming and domesticating livestock. Each settlement had its own distinct culture, customs, and traditions. They were characterized by the painted pottery and jade carvings they produced.

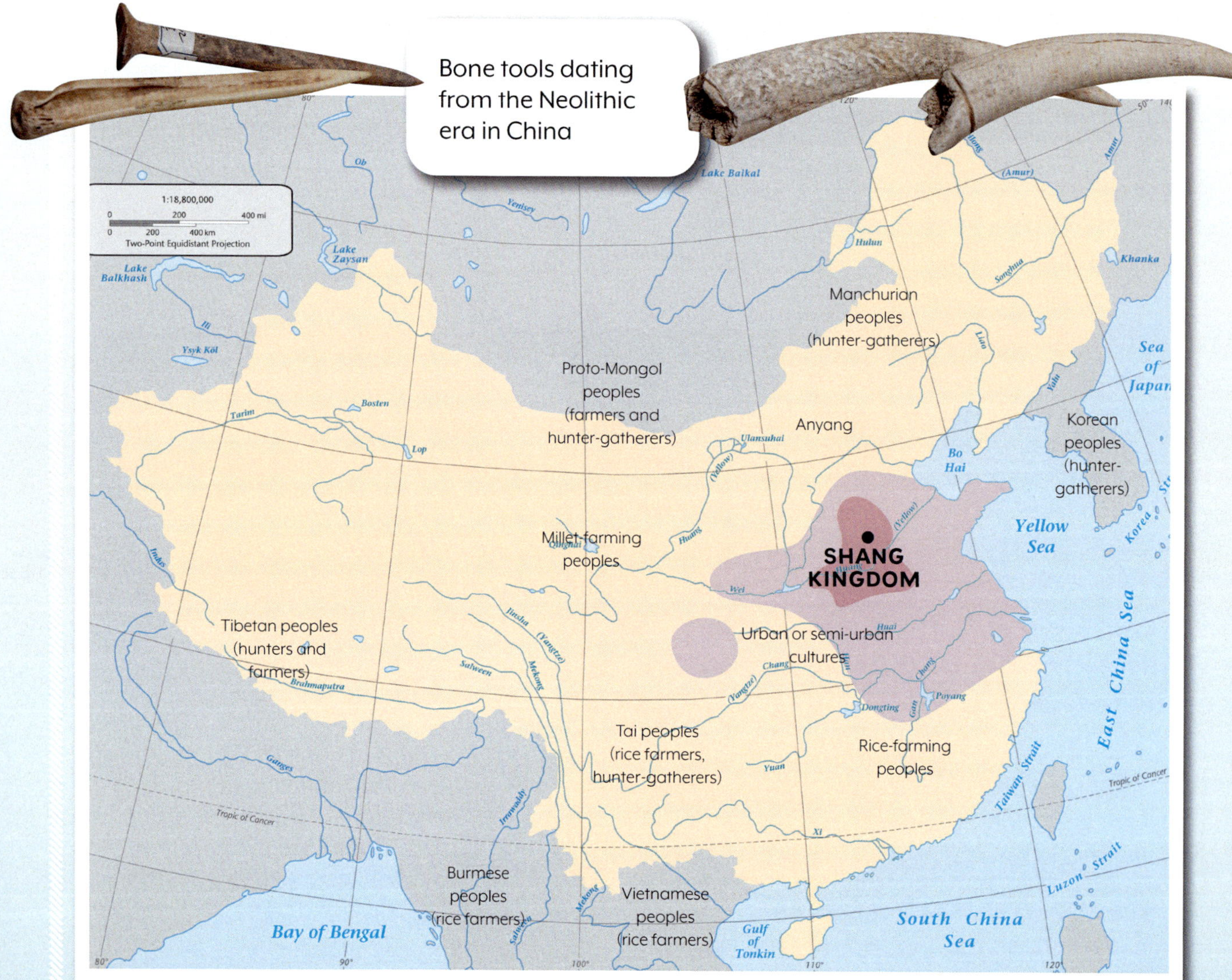

Bone tools dating from the Neolithic era in China

The Guyaju Caves are cave dwellings northwest of Beijing. They are thought to have been made by the Kumo Xi people and date from 207 C.E. to 907 C.E. The Kumo Xi were descendants of ancient **nomadic** peoples of northern China.

Rise of Dynasties

As small villages began to spread across the land, some grew into cities. They developed a central form of government called a dynasty. In a dynasty, there are a series of rulers that all come from the same family. When the current ruler dies, the next family member in the line of **succession** takes their place. Usually, it is the oldest son.

The Xia dynasty was the first of many dynasties to rule over China. For 45 years, Yu the Great was ruler of this dynasty. He is credited with developing the concept of central government in China and establishing the notion of the dynasty. Before that time, rulers were chosen based on their skills and experience. When Yu died, his son Qi became the next ruler. The Xia ruled between 2070 B.C.E. and 1600 B.C.E.

Until the 1900s, there was no archaeological evidence that this dynasty ever existed. Historians then found artifacts that suggest it was real. However, many scholars believe that most of the tales surrounding the history of the Xia dynasty are myths.

Yu the Great as depicted by a later dynasty. Many early ancient emperors and kings such as Yu, and his predecessors the Three Sovereigns and Five Emperors, are considered mythical because there is no evidence to prove they existed.

Emperor Yao was one of the Three Sovereigns and Five Emperors of ancient China, whose mother was a goddess. He himself was a descendant of the Yellow Emperor, an early god.

Shang Dynasty

The Shang dynasty is the first dynasty mentioned in historical records to have firm archaeological evidence of its existence. It was founded around 1600 B.C.E. by Cheng Tang, who was the first of as many as 30 kings over the dynasty's 600 or so years in existence. The dynasty was located in the North China Plain. It stretched to what are now known as the Shandong and Hebei provinces in the north, and as far west as the modern-day Henan province. Farmers took advantage of the fertile soil along the banks of the Yellow River to produce ample food supplies.

The Yin Ruins are the site of an ancient capital city of the late Shang dynasty.

Many cultural and religious traditions were developed during the time of the Shang dynasty, such as **Taoism**. The Shang also worshiped a supreme god called Shangdi, as well as several lesser gods. People believed their ancestors developed special powers after they died, and they could call on them in times of need. They built complex tomb structures to honor the dead and performed rituals to their spirits. People believed the king was **appointed** by the gods and served as a link between the living and the dead.

Over time, the Shang dynasty began to decline. People lost faith in the last emperor, Di Xin, who was very cruel and more focused on satisfying his own needs than those of his people.

The tomb of Shang dynasty military general Fu Hao at the Yin Ruins dates to 1200 B.C.E.

A horse carved during the late Shang dynasty

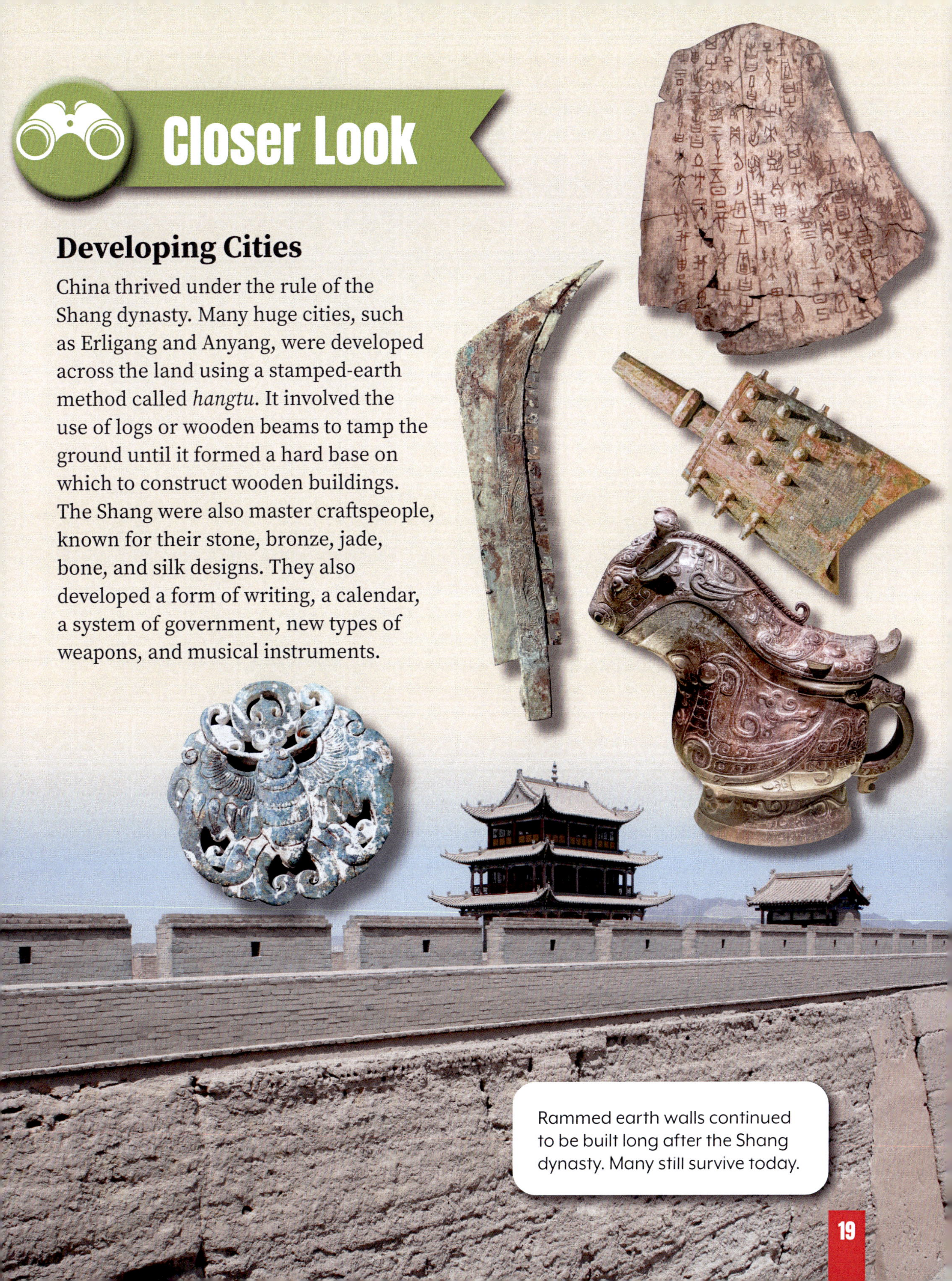

Closer Look

Developing Cities

China thrived under the rule of the Shang dynasty. Many huge cities, such as Erligang and Anyang, were developed across the land using a stamped-earth method called *hangtu*. It involved the use of logs or wooden beams to tamp the ground until it formed a hard base on which to construct wooden buildings. The Shang were also master craftspeople, known for their stone, bronze, jade, bone, and silk designs. They also developed a form of writing, a calendar, a system of government, new types of weapons, and musical instruments.

Rammed earth walls continued to be built long after the Shang dynasty. Many still survive today.

Zhou Dynasty

The Shang dynasty was overthrown in 1046 B.C.E. by the Zhou dynasty (1046–256 B.C.), which had long been established west of Shang lands in present-day Shaanxi province. The two dynasties had very similar cultures and practiced many of the same customs and rituals. However, at times they clashed and would go to war with each other. It was not until after the people of the Shang dynasty rebelled against their leaders that the Zhou dynasty gained control over China.

King Cheng of Zhou was the second king of the Chinese Zhou dynasty. He was a child when made king, so his uncle, the Duke of Zhou, supervised his government. The Duke established a capital city at Luoyang for the king.

Mandate of Heaven

The Zhou **invoked** a concept known as the Mandate of Heaven. They claimed the ruler of the land is given the role by a divine power or ancient god. According to the Mandate of Heaven, the ruler needs to use his power for good. If he becomes corrupt or treats people poorly, he will lose his power. The Zhou said the Shang did not deserve to continue to lead because they had become selfish and were not upholding the Mandate of Heaven. As a result, the Shang had lost favor with the gods. Because they were good, fair leaders, the Zhou said they should take control of the dynasty instead. Like the Shang, many future dynasties also fell on the basis of the Mandate.

An ancient bronze pan with inscriptions about the Zhou emperors

An ancient dragon-painted coffin is an artifact from a tomb dating from 481–221 B.C.E., during the Warring States Period.

Longest Dynasty

The Zhou dynasty was in power longer than any other Chinese dynasty. It was divided into two different periods and 37 different rulers. At first, the Western, or Xi, Zhou dynasty ruled from the capital near present-day Xi'an in western China. The focus fell away from the central government and turned to a system of **feudalism** instead. Under this system, the ruler granted relatives and nobles certain land rights. Peasants then worked the land of the feudal states. However, over the next few centuries, the feudal system began to break down. The king's power waned and conflicts arose between states.

In 771 B.C.E, the capital was relocated to Luoyang in eastern China, and the period of the Eastern, or Dong, Zhou dynasty, began. There was no strong leader during this time, and smaller states banded together to form several larger states that would then fight for control of China. The Warring States Period, as it became known, lasted from about 481 to 221 B.C.E., when a state called Qin claimed victory, and the Zhou dynasty collapsed.

Culturally, the Zhou mainly built on the developments of the Shang. Many other advancements occurred during their rule. They introduced ironworks, began riding horses, advanced Chinese warfare and weaponry, and began using ox-drawn plows. They developed irrigation systems to redirect floodwaters to their crops.

The Dujiangyan is an ancient irrigation and flood control system that dates back to the Qin era (256 B.C.E.). It still exists and functions today in Dujiangyan City, Sichuan province. The Min River was rechanneled to divide the water and irrigate 2,000 square miles (5,300 sq. km), making it the most productive agricultural region in China. The system was destroyed in a 1933 earthquake, but rebuilt.

Unifying China

The Qin dynasty was the shortest-lived in Chinese history. It was only in power for about 15 years, but it had great influence during that time. Under the rule of Qin Shi Huang, the dynasty established a government system—parts of which survive today. Until that time, China was made up of many warring kingdoms. The Qin ended hundreds of years of bloodshed by bringing the separate kingdoms together under a central system. It consisted of provinces governed by appointed leaders. In addition, the dynasty began to standardize the different systems of laws, writing, coinage, weights, and measurements that had been used across the land. Many of the systems developed by the Qin remained in place for centuries.

Along with a network of roads and canals, Qin Shi Huang ordered the construction of the original Great Wall of China. He is perhaps most famous for the army of thousands of terra-cotta warriors he had built to surround his tomb. The Qin dynasty fell apart after the death of the first emperor in 210 B.C.E. After years of harsh treatment and being forced to pay high taxes to fund the empire's projects, the people became upset and rebelled. China was reunited by the Han dynasty in 207 B.C.E.

The famous terra-cotta army is part of the **mausoleum** of the first emperor, Qin Shi Huang, who died in 210 B.C.E. His mausoleum took more than 36 years to complete, using 700,000 workers.

The Dahuting Tomb murals of the late Eastern Han dynasty (25–220 C.E.) that followed the Qin dynasty (221–207 B.C.E.). The tombs were the vaulted burial chambers of Zhang Boya, a powerful governor, and his wife. They were decorated to show scenes of daily life.

The Great Wall of China was built across the northern borders of several states of ancient China over several centuries. It is a series of defensive forts connected for thousands of miles by large walls of rammed earth, stones, wood, and later, bricks.

Last Empire

The period of unification that started with the Qin dynasty, known as Imperial China, remained fairly stable for hundreds of years. Many different empires ruled over Imperial China, and each had its own unique characteristics. The Qing dynasty came into power in 1644, and it was the last empire to rule over China. It spanned across the lands now known as China, Mongolia, and parts of Russia.

The Qing dynasty originated in Manchuria, which is in present-day northeastern China and eastern Russia. At the time, it was not part of China and the Chinese thought of the Qing as outsiders. The Qing were called in to help the Ming dynasty (1368–1644) maintain its power, but they conquered the Ming instead.

Also known as the Manchu, the Qing dynasty had a different culture, language, and traditions than the majority of the Chinese population it ruled over. However, once in power, the Qing adapted its leadership style to keep its multi-ethnic population content. It blended Manchu customs with government practices established by the previous dynasty.

The Ming dynasty (1368–1644) was known as the Great Ming. Their reign was a period of trade expansion throughout Asia and the West. Zhu Di (1360–1424) was the third Ming dynasty emperor. Called the Yongle Emperor, he was the most powerful Ming ruler. He moved the capital to Beijing and began construction on the Forbidden City.

A Ming vase dating from around the 1420s. Ming ceramics and porcelain, often with blue and white patterns, were prized in Europe.

The Forbidden City in Beijing is a group of 980 buildings formerly used as the residence of China's emperor. It was constructed from 1406 to 1420 and was the center of Chinese government over several dynasties for more than 500 years—but primarily the Ming.

Fall of Imperial China

At its peak, during the mid to late 1700s, the Qing dynasty was one of the most powerful empires in the world. The population more than doubled during this time, and the economy thrived thanks to domestic and foreign trade. But by the 1800s, China's power and influence began to decline. The Qing dynasty's government systems were outdated and could not match the pace of change. **Reforms** failed. Foreign pressure on China to trade with the West brought about wars and forced treaties that weakened government. Rebellions and revolts broke out.

Beginning in the 1860s, a series of three emperors died with either child **heirs** or no apparent heirs. The country was then effectively ruled by two women of the court. Empresses **Dowager** Cixi and Ci'an became regents for the Tongzhi and Guangu Emperors. China's last emperor, Puyi, or the Xuantong Emperor, was not yet three years old when he came to power in 1908. In the autumn of 1911, **revolutionaries** overthrew the Qing, and China's last dynasty ended.

Puyi

Empress Dowager Cixi was regent for two emperors during the Qing dynasty from 1861 until 1908. She introduced many reforms to help the dynasty cling to power, and died two days before China's last emperor, Puyi, came to power. Puyi was ousted, or removed, from power in 1912.

The Opium Wars were two wars (1839–1842 and 1856–1860) waged between China and Britain and France. Western countries wanted trading rights and control of Chinese territory. They engaged in smuggling opium—a powerful and addictive drug—from India into China. China tried to clamp down on the drug as many Chinese became addicted, and the wars were a result.

This sculpture honors the Silk Road at its starting point in Xi'an. The Silk Road was a number of trade routes through East and Southeast Asia that brought silk from China to other empires from 114 B.C.E. through 1450s C.E. The routes ran through isolated areas of deserts and mountains, which made China's trade more secure.

Closer Look

Trade and Turmoil

Because of its natural features and location, parts of what is now China remained largely isolated from the rest of the world for centuries. This helped protect it from nations that might want to invade—but still allowed Chinese traders to connect with outside markets. For centuries, China's emperors also tightly controlled trade within its borders and ocean ports, including who could trade and how. During the Qing dynasty, merchant groups called *hongs* managed trade through warehouses called "Canton factories." But foreign trading companies and countries wanted more favorable trade deals. Eventually, foreign discontent led to wars.

Republic of China

The revolution in 1911–1912 that ended dynasty rule in China was known as the Xinhai Revolution. It established the Republic of China. The next four decades were politically unstable. Political power changed frequently from one leader to another, often through conflict or violence. Throughout the 1920s, there were many clashes between **nationalist** and **communist** groups that led to a revolution.

In 1937, Japan invaded China. It had previously invaded much of northeastern China and wanted to expand its hold. The war lasted eight years and cost millions of lives. After it ended, a civil war continued to rage in China between the ruling Chinese Nationalist Party, or Kuomintang, and the Chinese Communist Party (CCP). It ended with a victory for the CCP in 1949.

Sun Yat-sen

Sun Yat-sen was elected as the **provisional** president of the Republic of China before handing power over to Yuan Shikai, a Qing leader. Yuan Shikai made himself an emperor of China in 1915—a title he held for just 83 days before revolts forced him to restore the republic.

People's Republic of China

Mao Zedong, leader of the CCP, announced the creation of the People's Republic of China on October 1, 1949. However, the government had no experience transitioning to a communist regime, so it looked to the **Union of Soviet Socialist Republics** (USSR) for help. The relationship that formed between these two nations would impact foreign relations between China and other countries that did not support communism, such as the United States, for decades to come.

Yuan Shikai

Mao Zedong was a communist revolutionary and founder of the People's Republic of China (PRC). He led it as chairman from 1949 until his death in 1976.

Cultural Revolution

The government continued making social, political, and land reforms. Rapid industrialization became one of the primary focuses. The concept of landlords was abolished, or officially ended, and land was redistributed to peasants. Over time, peasants were pressured to join rural farming **collectives**, and much of the land was returned to the state as a result. The goal of collectivization further advanced China's industrialization by providing the funds to support it and also food to feed workers in the cities.

The CCP launched the Cultural Revolution in 1966. **Radicals** had started to rise up against the communist regime, which wanted to put them down. **Intellectuals**, as well as anyone with any ties to the West or the Kuomintang, were **persecuted**, abused, or even killed. The education system was overhauled, and cultural and historical relics, customs, and ideas were destroyed. The Cultural Revolution lasted until the death of Mao Zedong in 1976. Millions of people died or were displaced, and China's economy suffered.

The "Little Red Book" is a book of speeches, quotes, and writings by Mao Zedong published during the Cultural Revolution. The book was intended to be inspirational and the CCP's goal was that 99 percent of the country would read the book.

Propaganda posters and sayings that promoted the Cultural Revolution were common, with sayings painted on homes and other buildings.

CHAPTER 3 Life Today

Farmers in a rice field harvest using ancient practices.

A factory worker in the city of Tangshan adjusts a spinning line in a modern textile factory.

After the death of Mao Zedong, China began to transition into its present-day form. Leaders, such as Deng Xiaoping, Jiang Zemin, and Hu Jintao, sought to create a **socialist market economy.** This shift in focus helped China become one of the fastest-growing economies. It grew by about 10 percent each year for about 30 years. At the end of World War II, in 1945, China was one of the poorest countries in the world. By 2011, it was the second-largest economy in the world after the United States. Today, China is the world's largest **exporter** and the second-biggest **importer**.

Communism and Government

Today, the CCP appoints the leaders of all state-owned enterprises, as well as all government leaders. Whoever runs the CCP also runs the country. This means the country's top leader is the general secretary of the ruling CCP party. This person is also the president, chief of state, and military commander.

The president and vice president are at the top of the executive branch of the government. They are elected by the legislative branch, which is called the National People's Congress. They serve five-year terms for up to two consecutive terms.

Container ships being loaded at port. Today, China is the leading manufacturer of shipping equipment. It has the world's second-largest fleet of commercial shipping vessels. About 48 percent of the world's shipbuilding orders are made in China.

To increase steel production across the country, the CCP encouraged the use of backyard furnaces to melt metal objects into steel. Forests were also cut down as fuel for the furnaces.

The president appoints the premier, who is the second most powerful person in China. This person is the head of government, which is called the State Council. The National People's Congress is the highest form of state power in China. It consists of about 2,980 members who are elected to five-year terms by voters in China.

Legal System

China uses a system of law that is based on a mix of Soviet and European legal systems. In May 2020, the National People's Congress passed its Civil Code, which is the longest piece of legislation in the history of the People's Republic of China. It signified a major step forward for China's legal system and strengthened civil rights across the country. There are four levels of courts in China. There are about 3,000 basic people's courts that try civil and criminal cases at the local level.

Closer Look

Great Leap Forward

Between 1958 and 1962, the Chinese government carried out a campaign called the Great Leap Forward. This was an attempt to remake the country into a communist society by increasing both agricultural yields and industry such as steel production. In rural areas, people were forced to work on collective farms. At first, community kitchens were built to serve food to laborers, but with so many people also forced to work on industrial projects, fields were not well tended and many crops rotted. A massive **famine** resulted, and millions of people died of starvation. Others were beaten or tortured to death.

The National People's Congress has the power to make decisions on major issues and put laws into effect. Provincial governments are on par with the central government. They implement policies developed by the central government and also develop their own.

Industry and Labor

From 1911 to 1978, most businesses in China were owned or controlled by the state. Today, state-owned enterprises (SOEs) account for less than half of the industrial output in China. The services sector is the largest sector. It accounts for about 54 percent of the country's economy. It includes health care, finance, hospitality, retail, entertainment, transportation, and recreation.

Manufacturing is the second-largest sector in China, accounting for about 38 percent of the country's wealth. Steel, chemicals, cement, toys, aircraft, and textiles are just a few of the many products China manufactures. China is a major exporter of goods around the world, including electronics, furniture, footwear, plastics, vehicles, machinery, and much more. However, the manufacturing industry has been declining in recent years, down more than 7 percent since 2010.

A virtual reality games expo in Beijing shows off some of the new technology designed and built in China.

Players at a games café in the city of Chongqing

Workers lift and check a solar panel on a production line of a factory in central China.

In some rural areas, ethnic minorities still follow ancient farming practices.

Agriculture

China's third-largest sector is agriculture, even though only about 10 percent of the land is suitable for farming. In addition, much of the land is at risk of droughts, erosion, and flooding. Still, agriculture makes up about 8 percent of the economy, and about 300 million people work in this industry. Most work on small-scale farms that use hand tools instead of advanced machinery. Some of the most common farm products in China include wheat, rice, corn, soybeans, cotton, tobacco, and peanuts. The country is also one of the world's largest producers of aquaculture, poultry, eggs, and pigs.

Although there is a great deal of potential for the mining and energy sectors, they remain fairly underdeveloped. China has yet to explore many of its rich mineral deposits and oil and natural gas reserves.

A worker at an aquaculture farm feeds grouper fish.

China is one of the top wheat producers in the world.

Education

China has a global reputation for excellence when it comes to its education system. It is mandatory for kids to receive a basic nine-year education. Kids start school at age six and must attend six years of primary school and three years of middle school. After that, they can attend three more years of high school at either a regular high school, a high school that focuses on vocational studies, or a high school that focuses on career and professional studies.

In cities, schools are funded by the state and provide a high-quality education. However, in rural areas, schools are often understaffed. Resources are limited and education quality is not as good. Many schools focus on providing vocational training due to the lack of spots at the university level.

Children attend school from about 8 a.m. to 5 p.m., five days a week, from September through June.

Schools place a strong emphasis on discipline and have strict rules. They often assign large amounts of homework.

Students eat at the cafeteria of a middle school in Jiangxi province.

Traditional Chinese Medicine (TCM) for sale at a market in Xishuangbanna, Yunnan province. TCM is a thriving industry that uses ancient knowledge and over 1,000 plant and 36 animal species as medicinal aids. Conservation organizations have condemned the trade in wild animals sometimes used in TCM.

Health Care

China believes in basic medical care as a human right for all citizens of the country. As such, the country has a health care program that provides free basic medical services to everyone who needs them without charge. Traditional Chinese medicine is also widely practiced across the country. Its roots go back more than 2,000 years and are focused on understanding the body's *qi* or life-force. It includes using medicines made from plants, minerals, and animals as well as practices that keep the body healthy, such as acupuncture, massage, and cupping.

China's central government is responsible for legislation related to health care, and local governments are responsible for providing health care services.

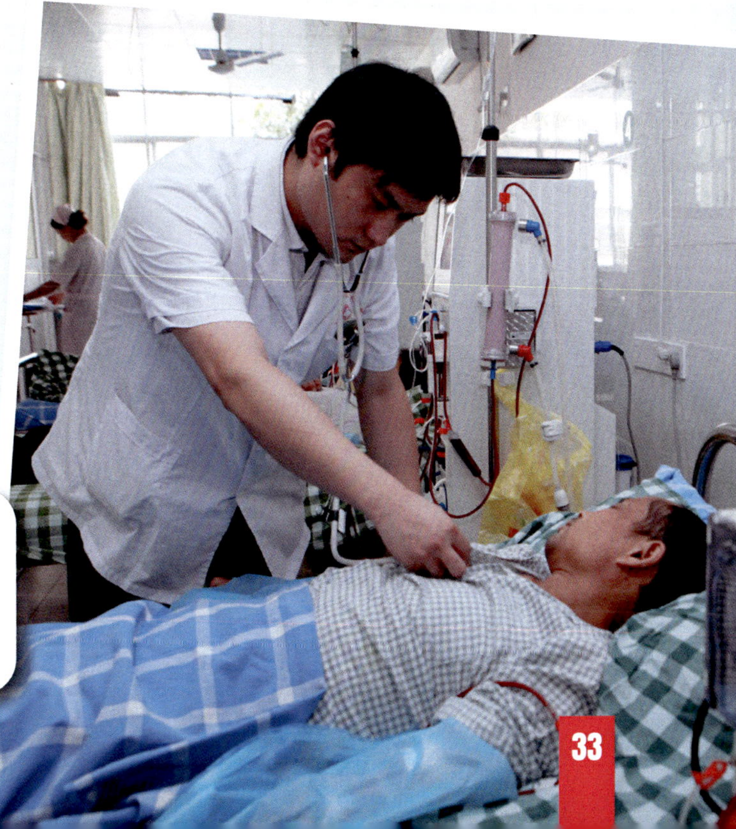

CHAPTER 4

A Vibrant Culture

Being isolated from the rest of the world for so many centuries, China developed a culture, customs, and traditions that were influenced by ancient **philosophies** and ways of life. It is also a country with 56 officially recognized ethnic groups. Although there are similarities from one ethnic group and region to another, there are also unique features that make each one distinct.

China reached its population peak in 2022 at 1.426 billion. The population is now declining. Ninety-two percent of Chinese people belong to the Han ethnic group, which is also the world's largest ethnic group.

Society

At its core, China is a collectivist culture, and everyone is encouraged to live in harmony despite differences. This concept officially promotes the good of the collective people over one's own individual needs. In public, Chinese people will often stay silent or remain impassive even if they disagree with something. Tone of voice, facial expression, and body language is important in communication. They try to create a sense of harmony so as not to embarrass anyone publicly. However, in recent decades, individualism is becoming more common.

China's written language dates back about 6,000 years, making it the oldest in the world. Even though people speak many dialects across China, they have a common written language.

Language is the main way to differentiate ethnic groups. There are seven main Chinese dialects but more than 70 percent of people in China speak Mandarin, or Putonghua, dialect. Other common dialects include Yue (Cantonese), Xiang (Hunanese), Min, Gan, Wu, and Hakka (Kejia). China's minority groups also have their own spoken languages.

Closer Look

Nation and Ethnicities

China's population is mostly homogenous and the vast majority of people are Han. Han people originated along the Yellow River in northern China. They share a culture, values, written language, and traditions, but they speak a wide range of dialects. In addition to the Han, the Chinese government officially recognizes 55 ethnic minority groups. Most are located in the southwestern, northwestern, and northeastern parts of the country. In some areas, ethnic groups make up a significant part or a majority of the population. They have different languages, cultures, religions, and histories.

As China expanded its control over these areas, it introduced a Regional Ethnic Autonomy System. Officially, this was to make ethnic minorities a part of China's political system, and protect their rights. In reality it has removed their ability to fully govern themselves and to express their cultural identities. The five autonomous regions are Inner Mongolia, Xinjiang, Guangxi, Ningxia, and Tibet. Tibet is 86.6 percent Tibetan and Xinjiang is 45 percent Uyghur. China expects these regions to accept that they are part of a unitary state of China.

A Uyghur family eats at a market in Kashgar in this pre-2014 photo.

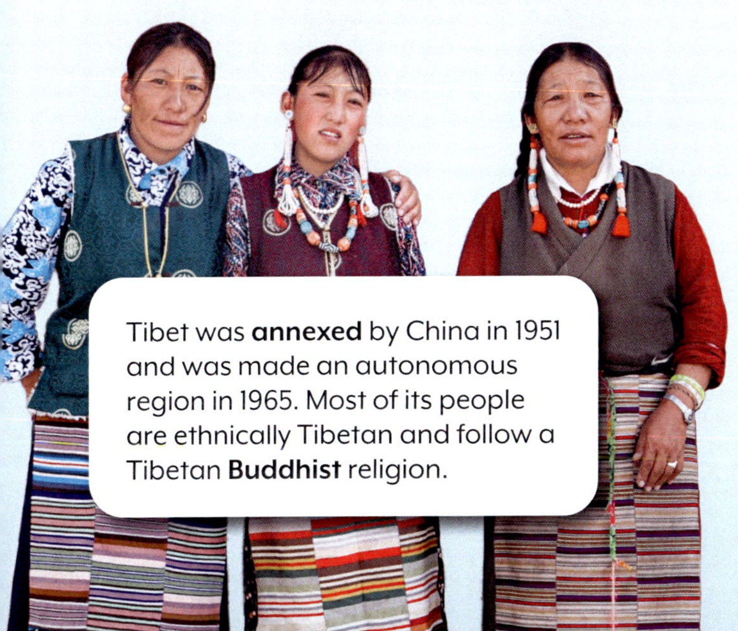

Tibet was **annexed** by China in 1951 and was made an autonomous region in 1965. Most of its people are ethnically Tibetan and follow a Tibetan **Buddhist** religion.

Uyghurs

Uyghurs are an ethnic group in China's northwestern Xinjiang Uyghur Autonomous Region. They are **Turkic** peoples native to this area and speak a Turkic language. They also follow Islam. Uyghurs make up the majority of the population in Xinjiang. Human rights organizations have documented rights abuses against the Uyghurs by the Chinese state. These include the detention of over a million in internment camps since 2014, the tracking and **reeducation** of Uyghurs, and **genocide**. The Chinese government denies this and has claimed it is cracking down on terrorism.

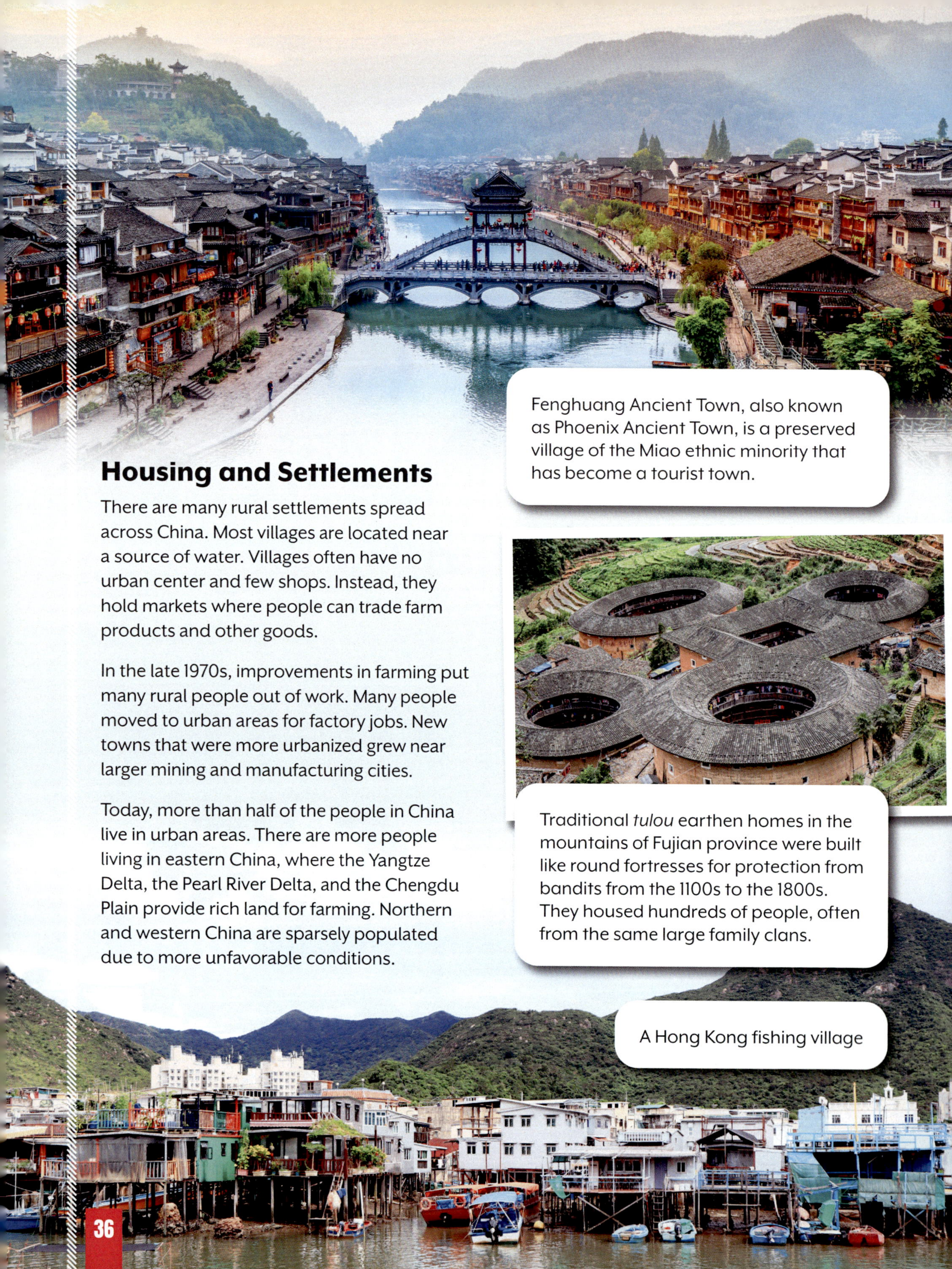

Fenghuang Ancient Town, also known as Phoenix Ancient Town, is a preserved village of the Miao ethnic minority that has become a tourist town.

Housing and Settlements

There are many rural settlements spread across China. Most villages are located near a source of water. Villages often have no urban center and few shops. Instead, they hold markets where people can trade farm products and other goods.

In the late 1970s, improvements in farming put many rural people out of work. Many people moved to urban areas for factory jobs. New towns that were more urbanized grew near larger mining and manufacturing cities.

Today, more than half of the people in China live in urban areas. There are more people living in eastern China, where the Yangtze Delta, the Pearl River Delta, and the Chengdu Plain provide rich land for farming. Northern and western China are sparsely populated due to more unfavorable conditions.

Traditional *tulou* earthen homes in the mountains of Fujian province were built like round fortresses for protection from bandits from the 1100s to the 1800s. They housed hundreds of people, often from the same large family clans.

A Hong Kong fishing village

Traditional Housing

Upon the establishment of the People's Republic of China in 1949, property owners could only keep the portion of their homes that they needed to accommodate their families. The rest was taken over by the state and distributed among the general population. Traditionally, the types of housing people lived in depended on the geographic location and weather conditions. Wood was hard to come by in northern China. People built homes from sun-dried bricks, tamped mud, or stone. In southern China, people used brick, wood, and bamboo to build their homes.

City Living

Today, apartments are the most common form of housing in China. Most are state-owned and provided to people by their workplace. Local governments provide housing for people who are not part of a workplace. Since 1978, private ownership has been encouraged, and people can purchase their own housing if they have the means.

Many homes in China do not have central heating, and they can get quite cold in winter. People often sleep in long underwear or layers to stay warm. In the north, where it gets especially cold, people sleep on raised beds called *kangs*. They are built over a stove or fireplace.

Massive blocks of apartments are common in China's large cities such as Kunming.

Shanghai is the third most populous city in the world, with around 24 million residents. It is also a city of finance, business, and research, and a showcase for China's new economy where many very wealthy people live.

CHAPTER 4

Religion

China is the birthplace of several ancient belief systems. Confucianism, or Ruism, is a philosophy and world view developed from the teachings of Chinese philosopher Confucius (551–479 B.C.E.). Many of his teachings, which focus on the importance of family, harmony, and moral goodness, are still followed and respected by people in China. Taoism is another ancient Chinese philosophy that teaches living in harmony and balance. China was an early adopter of Buddhism after it was introduced to the country 2,000 years ago. Starting in 1949, the Chinese Communist Party declared China an **atheist** country. Some religions were persecuted and others were closely monitored.

Today, Chinese people officially have the freedom of religious belief. In practice, that freedom is challenged and believers are persecuted when any religion or belief system is seen as a threat to the control and beliefs of the state. About half the population is atheist or does not practice a religion. There are five official religions recognized by the Chinese government—Buddhism, Taoism, Islam, Catholicism, and Protestantism.

Yin and yang is an ancient Chinese philosophical idea that explains how the world is interconnected with both dark and light sides. It is represented by half-circle figures that swirl into each other.

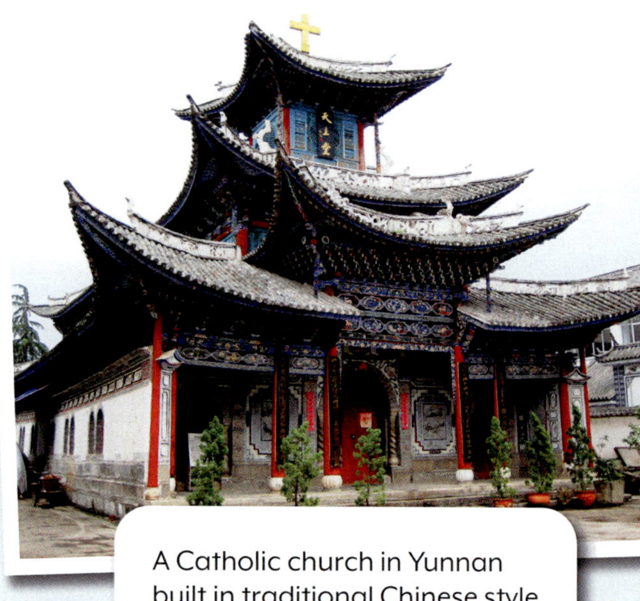

A Catholic church in Yunnan built in traditional Chinese style

The Longmen Grottoes in Henan are examples of ancient Buddhist cave art in China. They were carved from 493 C.E. to 1127 C.E.

Family Celebrations

Across China, people participate in many festivals and celebrations to express their culture and heritage. The Spring Festival, or Lunar New Year, is one of the best-known and most important. It brings together families to ring in the new year and honor their ancestors and gods. It takes place from the first through the fifteenth day of the first **lunar month** each year.

The Dragon Boat Festival is another important celebration. It occurs on the fifth day of the fifth lunar month and commemorates the death of Qu Yuan, a famous Chinese poet. The Mid-Autumn Festival, or Moon Festival, celebrates the harvest and gives thanks for the bounty. It happens on the fifteenth day of the eighth lunar month, when the moon is the fullest and brightest of the autumn season. Winter Solstice commemorates the shortest day and longest night of the year. It falls between December 21 and 23.

During the Dragon Boat Festival, people race dragon boats and throw *zongzi*, or dumplings, into the river as a sacrifice to the Dragon God.

Food and Fun

Traditional Chinese festivals are celebrated by eating special foods, making decorations, and often wearing traditional or special clothing. Fireworks and red clothing are common at Lunar New Year. Paper lanterns are lit at lantern festivals held in spring. Special foods are made and shared with family and friends—and even the dead! The Hungry Ghost Festival, or Zhongyuan Festival, celebrated on the 15th day of the seventh lunar month, is when people remember and honor the dead and their ghosts. The food is left at altars to please the dead.

Tangyan are rice balls or sweet dumplings served during spring festivals.

Mooncakes are eaten at family gatherings during the Mid-Autumn Festival. These are round cakes with fillings such as fruit, cream, egg, or ham.

Workers enjoy a communal meal at a ceremony marking the construction of a new farmhouse in Guizhou province.

Everyday Staples

Rice or wheat-based foods are always served at meals. They are both staple foods grown in China, and rice or noodles accompany most meals. Other staple foods include bean sprouts, cabbage, and scallions. Meat is quite costly, so people don't always eat it daily. Chicken and pork are the most common forms of protein. Fish and seafood are also common. Food reflects different regions and cultures of China. For example, Shanghai is known for its seafood dishes. Cantonese foods are often sweet and include stir-fried foods. Dim sum, a combination of small appetizers, is common for lunch or breakfast. Sichuan is known for spicy foods cooked with peanuts, ginger, and sesame paste. Smoked duck and frog legs are common dishes. At home, most people in China eat from a bowl or small plate using chopsticks.

Farmers harvesting sweet potatoes in north China. Sweet potatoes are a staple food in China.

What to Wear?

Walk down a street in a Chinese city today and you may see teens wearing oversized hoodies and jeans, women in the latest French designer clothing, and men in tailored business suits. China is both a very modern and very ancient country and the clothing people wear every day and for special occasions represents this. Traditional Chinese clothing is loose and long. It evolved over China's 3,000-year history. Peasants wore clothing made from dark-colored hemp or cotton. The wealthy and members of the Imperial court wore silk. Silk originated in China in about 5000 B.C.E. For thousands of years, it was the only place silk could be bought, and was a highly prized trade item. Chinese emperors were known to never wear the same clothing twice.

Hanfu is the best-known and oldest style of Chinese clothing. It comes from the Han culture and is still sometimes worn by both men and women. It consists of a loose-fitting jacket with either pants or a skirt or a one-piece dress that is closed with a sash instead of buttons. During the early years of communism, many people adopted unisex Zhongshan suits consisting of simple cotton military-style jackets and loose-fitting pants.

Silkworm cocoons

China is still the world's largest producer of silk.

Older men in Zhongshan suits

Hanfu is sometimes worn for special events.

Arts and Entertainment

Many historic works of art considered too Western or decadent were destroyed, damaged, or banned during the Cultural Revolution. In recent decades, people have worked to restore the arts across China. Historically, painting, **calligraphy**, and poetry were popular among China's elite. The written word was also highly valued during ancient times, and there are many historical and literary accounts. Pottery, bronze work, sculptures, and carved **reliefs** have been found all over the country. Sculptures of Buddha are especially abundant throughout the countryside.

Song and dance have a long history in China. Archaeologists have discovered ancient instruments and pottery depicting dancers and musicians. Traditional instruments include the *erhu*, *sanxian*, *dongxiao*, *dizi*, and ceremonial gongs. Traditionally, theater and opera were also popular in China. People used performance art to tell stories about historical events, wars, and important activities. Today, China's entertainment industry is enormous, with revenue of more than $500 billion a year. It is a leader in virtual reality gaming, and its film industry has been producing highly-acclaimed *wuxia* martial arts films for decades. Wuxia is a film style that uses fast-paced martial arts, acrobatics, and stunts to tell stories of heroes and villains.

Mount Cangyan in Hebei province is a scenic area used in the film *Crouching Tiger, Hidden Dragon*, an award-winning martial arts movie made in 2000. It kicked off a broad interest in wuxia martial art films outside of Asia.

Traditional Chinese opera is a form of musical theater that dates back thousands of years. Known for its vibrant makeup, clothing, dance, and use of traditional stringed orchestra instruments, it was the main form of cultural entertainment until the 1900s. Today, several professional opera companies still tour the country and the world.

Martial Arts

Martial arts are an important part of Chinese culture, and descriptions of them date back 4,000 years, when soldiers would practice hand-to-hand combat and defense techniques. Chinese kung fu was developed during the Shang and Zhou dynasties. Today, there are many different styles of kung fu, including Taijiquan, Shaolin, and Qigong. It is common for people to gather together in parks and other public spaces to practice martial arts each day.

Terra-cotta warriors from the Qin dynasty

Cultural Institutions and Sites

Beijing is the cultural hub of China. It is home to the Chinese Academy of Sciences, National Archives Administration of China, and National Library of China. It is also where the Palace Museum is located, which includes the Forbidden City that served as the political center of the Ming and Qing dynasties.

The Forbidden City is one of more than 2,300 cultural relics now under state protection across China. These relics include many cultural and historical sites that are deemed to be of significant value at the national level. Others include the Great Wall and the mausoleum of Emperor Qin Shi Huang. There are also many relics and sites that have been protected at the provincial and local levels. There are 50 UNESCO World Heritage Sites in China, which is more than any other country in the world, except Italy.

Shaolin monks demonstrate their Shaolin Wusho form of kung fu at a training temple in Luoyang, Henang province. Luoyang is one of China's oldest cities.

CHAPTER 5 Looking to the Future

The People's Republic of China moved from being one of the world's poorest countries to one of the wealthiest in a span of less than 100 years. The Chinese Civil War (1927–1949) and the changes made during the early years of communism devastated the economy. In the late 1970s, the Chinese Communist Party (CCP) began making new economic reforms that encouraged private business, foreign investment, and special economic zones. The reforms created Chinese **state capitalism**, where the CCP maintains control of the state, the people, and the economy, but business flourishes. Today, China is the largest trading nation in the world—with the largest manufacturing economy. It is also the second-largest importer of goods worldwide.

Billionaires Club

Today, China ranks second in the world for the number of billionaires—at nearly 500. All are businesspeople who made fortunes in the manufacturing, food, finance, energy, technology, health care, and real estate industries. China has produced billionaires faster than any other country, and the country's middle class has also grown. The government has pledged to eliminate poverty, but 600 million people still live on $150 a month.

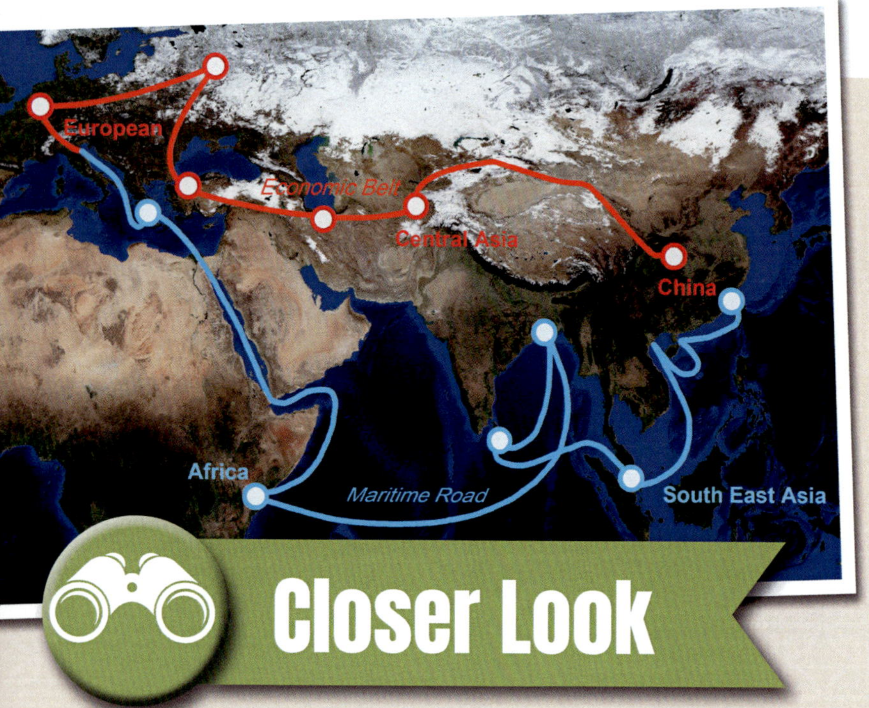

Closer Look

Controlling Trade

China's One Belt One Road project, or Belt and Road Initiative (BRI), is a global plan to build transportation networks such as roads, bridges, rail lines and ports throughout the world. It was launched in 2013 as a way for China to take a greater leadership role in trade and international affairs. Dozens of countries could benefit from funding to build new transportation routes and infrastructure. However, some countries, such as India and Japan, have questioned China's motives for the project. They worry what will happen if countries take on large debts to fund their portion of the project and then can't repay those debts. Over the past few decades, China has invested heavily in developing strategic transportation networks throughout Asia, Central Asia, and Africa.

This village in Sichuan province is part of China's Targeted Poverty Alleviation campaign. The CCP is working on raising incomes in rural areas and improving housing and services.

Climate change has made flooding worse in low-lying coastal cities. China's National Strategy on Climate Adaptation aims at transitioning to a low-carbon economy.

Future Challenges

In recent years, China has been battered by extreme weather conditions related to climate change. These include severe heat waves, floods, droughts, and forest fires, which have cost both lives and billions of dollars. Urban flooding alone is predicted to cost $77 billion a year by 2030. In addition, about 1.8 to 2 million people die in China each year due to the extreme pollution in the air.

Much of China relies on fossil fuels, such as coal, to fuel industry and daily life. In fact, China contributes about one-third of global greenhouse gas emissions.

Population Change

China has seen a lot of change in a short amount of time. Its ability to adapt to change on a large scale shows that it can continue to manage future challenges. For decades, China's population grew so much that the state imposed laws for population control. From 1979 to 2015, the one-child policy restricted most families to one child. This impacted the culture, economy, and **demographics** of the country. China's population started to decline in 2022. The policy worked to slow population growth, but it also means that China has an aging population today. China is now allowing larger families of up to three children. This shift is needed to ensure the country has enough workers and to fund pensions for retired people.

The one-child policy had consequences. Many families preferred to have boys instead of girls because boys carried on the family line. Many girls and disabled boys were put up for adoption or left at orphanages. As a result, there are many more males than females in China today.

administrative Related to the running or management of a country

annex To take or add a territory to another

appoint To assign a role or position to someone

atheist Does not believe in the existence of gods

autonomous Has the freedom to govern itself

Buddhist Relating to Buddhism, a religion based on the teachings of the Buddha, founded in India about 2,500 years ago

calligraphy A decorative style of writing

carbon emissions Gases such as carbon dioxide released into Earth's atmosphere by burning fossil fuels

ceded Gave up control

climate change A long-term change in the temperatures and weather patterns on Earth. Climate change often refers to global warming.

collective People who work together as a group rather than individually

communist Related to communism, an economic and political system in which goods and resources are owned commonly, usually by government, rather than by private individuals

deforestation The intentional cutting down of forests

demographics Statistics relating to the characteristics of human populations

density A measurement of how many people live in a specific area

desertification The process of how land becomes desert, such as through drought or deforestation

dialect A form of language that is specific to a region or social group

dowager A widow who holds a title or property from her deceased husband

economic Relating to the use, distribution, and production of resources, goods, and services

ethnically homogenous Made up of people who are connected by the same ethnicity

exporter A country, person, or company that sends goods to another country

famine Extreme and widespread food shortage

feudalism A social system in which people were granted protection and use of land by high-ranking landholders

genetically altered Plants or animals whose genes have been changed

genocide The intentional destruction of a people in whole or in part

Han people An East Asian ethnic group that makes up 92 percent of people in China

heirs People inheriting or continuing a legacy of an ancestor

hydroelectric resources Moving water that can be used to make electric power

importer A country, person, or company that brings in goods from other countries

industrialized Changed from mostly agricultural to more industrial

intellectuals Very educated or highly intelligent people

intrusion The movement of something where it doesn't belong

invoke To call on or bring about something

lunar month The period of time that it takes for the moon to pass through all of its phases

mausoleum A building that houses a person's remains

monsoon Seasonal winds that blow in off bodies of water and bring rain

nationalist A person or group that supports a strong independent state or government

Neolithic Period of human civilization beginning about 12,000 years ago; also called the New Stone Age

nomadic Moving from place to place

persecuted Systematic mistreatment of an individual or group, often because of their ethnicity, race, or religion

philosophies Truths, ways of living, or knowledge

populous Having a lot of people living there

provisional Something that exists for the present but might change later

radicals People who push for social or political change

reeducation The act of trying to change a person's beliefs

reforms Changes that improve social, economic, or political situations

reliefs Sculptures attached to a wall or solid background

republic A form of government where the state is ruled by representatives of the people and not a monarch

revolutionaries People who use force to overthrow the government

socialist market economy A type of economic system used by the People's Republic of China where the state owns all or part of most businesses but many operate like private firms in an economy controlled by the state

state capitalism An economic system where the state controls most businesses and the economy, extracting profits

succession The act of Inheriting a title from someone who comes before you

Taoism A Chinese system of philosophy, religion, and way of life developed by philosopher Lao Tzu around 500 B.C.E.

topography The features in an area of land, such as mountains and rivers

Turkic Relating to a collection of ethnic groups of Central, East, West, and North Asia, as well as parts of Europe, who speak Turkic languages

UNESCO World Heritage Site A protected landmark or area singled out by the United Nations Educational, Scientific, and Cultural Organization as being globally significant

Union of Soviet Socialist Republics A group of communist countries in Europe and Eurasia that existed from 1922 to 1991

Books

Bardoe, Cheryl. *China: A History*. Abrams Books, 2018.

Branscombe, Allison. *All About China: Stories, Songs, Crafts and Games for Kids*. Tuttle Publishing, 2018.

Oachs, Emily Rose. *Ancient China*. Bellwether Media, 2020.

Websites

https://cybersleuth-kids.com/sleuth/History/Ancient_Civilizations/China/
Learn more about ancient China.

www.cia.gov/the-world-factbook/countries/china
Stay current on the latest facts and figures about China.

www.britannica.com/place/China
Find out more about the land, culture, people, and history of China.

About the Author

Heather C. Hudak has written hundreds of kids' books on all kinds of topics. She loves to travel when she's not writing. Heather has visited about 60 countries, including China. While in China she climbed the Great Wall, practiced tai chi with hundreds of locals in a park, ate dim sum, and marveled at the terra-cotta warriors at Emperor Qin Shi Huang's mausoleum.